STITCHING THROUGH THE SEASONS

Evocative Patterns and Projects to Capture the Magic of Each Month

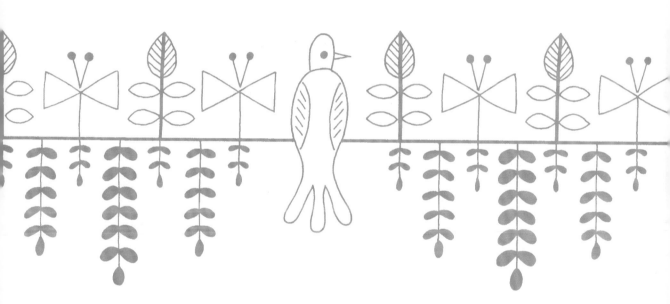

YUMIKO HIGUCHI

ROOST BOOKS

Contents

Note: Any and all of the projects included in this book are prohibited from commercial use or sale. Please enjoy handcrafting them for your own purposes.

Introduction

This collection of embroidery patterns takes the seasons as its theme. Throughout the course of my day-to-day life, I treasure the feast of the senses offered by the seasons. And in my creative work as well, each and every sketch and each and every stitch evokes the constantly changing seasons.

There may be cheerful, peaceful moments to enjoy, as well as harsh rain, wind, and extreme temperatures to endure. There will be events to look forward to and sudden sorrows to bear. Even amid the casual repetition of everyday life, there is so much to anticipate in the seasons, and I alternate between sketching and working on my creations with a pleasure that nourishes me.

Within these pages I have collected winsome and practical patterns and projects, including twelve months' worth of flowers and greenery, items and ephemera, some of which were part of a yearlong series that appeared in the magazine *Misesu*. To complete the array, there are numerical crests and emblems for each month, offering a rich assortment of ideas.

Although these embroidery projects require only your hands and fingertips, it's my hope that when you take the time to find the sweet rhythm of working stitches, they will gently inspire your mind and body with the abundance of the seasons.

—YUMIKO HIGUCHI

January

Start the new year with crisp and
clean motifs for the season.

Narcissus | page 62

Spring Herbs | page 68

Happy New Year | page 69

Pansies | page 70

February

The season of bitter cold. The dazzlingly vivid hue of these
flowers hints that spring's arrival is not far off.

Plum Blossoms | page 62

Spring Birds | page 71

Bird and Plant Pattern | page 72

This project uses the Bird and Plant Pattern, which imagines the dream of a little bird eagerly awaiting the coming spring. The vertical pattern is perfect for making a bag to carry long, tall items such as a wine bottle.

Wine Bag | page 73, 93

March

Beginning with tender yet hardy dandelions, here are patterns
for flowers that soak up spring's welcome rays of sunshine.

Dandelions | page 63

Tulips | page 73

Mimosas │ page 73

Mimosas are arrayed around a white, store-bought handkerchief. Setting them off against a white, black, or gray monotone fabric creates a neat and tidy effect. Use as a table centerpiece or as a basket cover.

Handkerchief | page 73

April

April is when spring is in full bloom, so we begin with a crest that
pairs an egg with rabbits to represent fertility and new life.

Easter Bunny | page 63

Cherry-Blossom Viewing | page 74

Spring Pressed Flowers | page 75

May

Such a bright and pleasant season of refreshing breezes. A time
for motifs with glorious flowers and fresh greenery.

Poppies | page 64

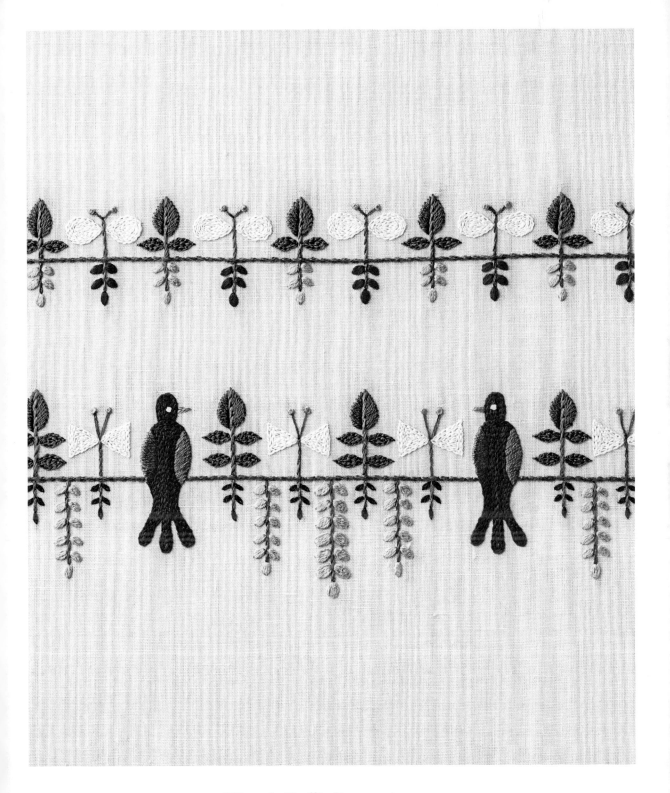

Wisteria Trellis Pattern | page 76

Spring Flower Pattern | page 78

New leaves highlight the season in verdant shades of fresh green, captured perfectly within an embroidery hoop in this wreath design.

Fresh Green Wreath | page 77

June

With umbrellas, hydrangea, and lavender swaying in the wind,
June's patterns call to mind the earth when it is rich and moist.

Rainy Season | page 64

Hydrangea | page 80

Lavender | page 81

Arranging the Lavender pattern horizontally
across an eye mask mimics a field of lavender. I
recommend filling it with lavender potpourri, so
that the fragrance can heighten your enjoyment.

Eye Mask | page 81, 94

July

With mystical coral, fish, and people frolicking in the
waves, here are motifs that conjure the sea.

Coral and Shell | page 65

School of Fish | page 80

Surfers | page 82

This fun cushion features surfers in their colorful
swimsuits arranged at random on a solid background.
Instructions for how to make a cushion are included,
but you can also use a store-bought pillow cover.

Cushion | page 82, 94

August

—

Liven up a tropical mood with plants and
fruits from a tropical climate.

Pineapple | page 65

Tropical Leaves | page 83

Summer Fruits | page 84

Embroider your favorite fruit from the
Summer Fruits pattern. All it requires is cutting
out fabric, so I recommend this project for
those who aren't confident about their sewing
skills. It also makes an excellent little gift.

Jar Cover | page 84, 95

September

Heading into the harvest season. With grapes and pears, pomegranates and ornamental berries, these motifs create a sense of abundance.

Grapes | page 66

Various shapes of purple flowers fill the edges of an embroidery hoop. Feel free to change up the colors of the flowers.

Purple Flowers | page 85

Autumn Fruits | page 86

40

Here, I scattered grapes from the Autumn Fruits pattern over a beret. The grapes can be worked freehand, which makes them perfect for materials that are difficult to trace patterns onto.

Beret | page 86

October

———

The arrival of full-fledged autumn.
With such a vibrant assortment of motifs, you can enjoy each and every stitch.

Pumpkin | page 66

Mushroom Wreath | page 87

Camping Gear | page 88

44

This autumnal display of fruit and flowers makes a lovely ornament out of a 4-inch embroidery hoop.

Pear and Flower Pattern | page 89

November

When the colors of the foliage deepen and it truly feels
like autumn, it's the perfect time to find cozy and warm
moments at home with your embroidery.

Teapot and Fallen Leaves | page 67

Sewing Tools | page 90

I used a mini cake tin to make this pincushion. You could also use an egg cup or a shot glass as a container. Choose your favorite item from the Sewing Tools pattern.

Pincushion | page 90

December

Lovely sprigs of mistletoe, subtly blooming Christmas roses, and snow. These motifs capture the spirit of the season.

Mistletoe | page 67

Snow Flower Pattern | page 91

A stocking filled with Christmas roses makes a
perfect holiday decoration. Use it to send all your
Christmas wishes to Santa on Christmas Eve.

Christmas Stocking | page 92, 95

Tools

A **Needles and Pincushion**
I use French embroidery needles with sharp points. The needle size depends on how many strands of embroidery floss are used.

B **Tailor's Shears**
It's best to have sharp shears that are specifically made for cutting fabric.

C **Eyeleteer**
Use this tool for perforations.

D **Tracer**
Use this tool to trace the pattern when transferring onto fabric. You can also use a ballpoint pen.

E **Embroidery Scissors**
Small, sharp, pointed scissors with a thin edge are the easiest to use.

F **Needle Threader**
This tool makes it easier to put the thread into the eye of a needle.

G **Tracing Paper**
This thin paper is one option for copying patterns.

H **Cellophane**
Use this material to transfer patterns onto fabric so that the tracing paper doesn't tear.

I **Chalk Paper**
Use this paper to transfer patterns onto fabric. For dark fabric, use white chalk paper.

J **Embroidery Hoops**
Use embroidery hoops to stretch fabric tightly. The hoop size will depend on the pattern size, but I recommend the smaller 4-inch hoop, since it's a comfortable size to hold when stitching.
Securely fasten your embroidery hoop. If your embroidery hoop is fastened too loosely, the fabric can sag and wrinkle. Take the time to wrap the inner hoop with bias tape or fabric (I recommend using white) to help prevent slippage. Once you've finishing wrapping the inner hoop, secure the end with a few stitches. When working with a larger pattern, you may need to slide the hoop over your work. To prevent delicate work from being damaged, place a patch of fabric over the embroidered section, then fit the hoop.

Materials

EMBROIDERY FLOSS

For all the projects in this book, I used No. 25 embroidery floss. Six-stranded floss is the most popular. I used DMC embroidery floss from France, which is known for its vivid colors and lustrous texture.

FABRIC

All of the projects here are made using linen. Plain-weave linen is easy to work with, can be washed, and has a smooth texture, so it's perfectly suited for embroidery fabric. It's best to wash linen before cutting it to size, then dry it away from direct sunlight. To readjust the fabric grain, iron the linen lightly before it's completely dry.

NUMBER OF STRANDS AND NEEDLE SIZE

Choose the size of your needle based on the number of strands you are using. By doing so, you'll always have the perfect needle for whatever project you're working on. The thickness of the fabric you're using also determines the size.

No. 25 Embroidery Floss	Embroidery Needle
6 strands	No. ¾
3–4 strands	No. 5/6
1–2 strands	Nos. 7–10

*These are standard sizes of Clover needles.

Basic Stitches and Embroidery Fundamentals

Here are nine basic embroidery stitches used in this book. I'll also show you tricks for finishing your work beautifully.

Straight Stitch

This stitch is for creating short lines. The number of strands you use will produce a different effect.

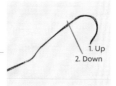

Running Stitch

This stitch creates a dotted line. Once you get the knack for this stitch, you can really run with it.

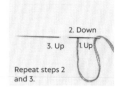

Outline Stitch

Use this for borders as well as for stems and branches. This stitch creates a beautiful finish when sewing on an intricate curve.

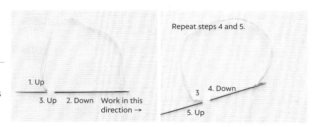

Chain Stitch

Use this stitch for lines or for filling in areas. To create a plump and pretty chain stitch, don't pull the thread too tight and keep the size of the loops uniform.

TIP

When filling in an area, be careful not to leave any gaps.

French Knot Stitch

The basic French knot stitch is a double wrap. Adjust the size based on the number of strands of thread. The knots are easily crushed, so work them as you finish a project.

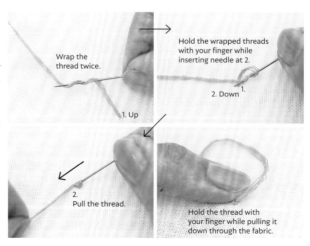

Satin Stitch

Work these stitches side by side to fill in an area. To create a beautiful finish, line up the parallel threads and make sure they aren't twisted.

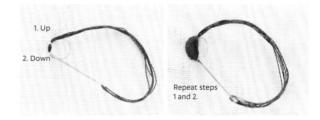

Long and Short Stitch

Work alternating long and short stitches side by side to fill in an area. Use this stitch for things such as fan-shaped flower petals.

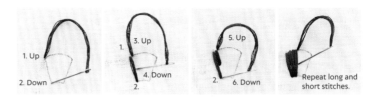

Lazy Daisy Stitch

This stitch creates a small flower petal or a leaf. Maintain a full shape by not pulling the thread too tightly.

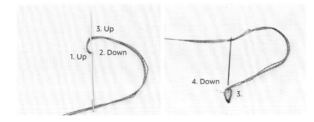

Lazy Daisy Stitch + Straight Stitch

Sew one or two straight stitches across the center of the lazy daisy. It creates a full oval shape. You can adjust the size depending on the number of strands.

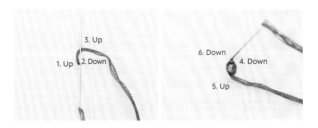

Making Beautiful Satin Stitches and Long and Short Stitches

When filling in the slightly complicated shapes of flower petals and leaves,
it's easier to create balance by starting your work from the center.

  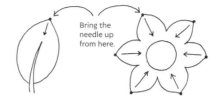

For flower petals, work stitches radially, starting from the outer line and working toward the center, to fill in the area. For leaves, work satin stitches starting from the center tip and working toward the center.

Tips for Chain Stitches
Filling In an Area Neatly (1)

Be careful not to leave any gaps.

1. Sew the outline of the pattern.

2. Following the outline; sew the additional rows, working from the outside toward the inside. If a gap appears, go back at the end and fill in with more chain stitches or outline stitches.

Filling In an Area Neatly (2)

How to embroider an area that also has an inner border:

 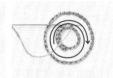

1. Sew both the outer and inner outlines of the pattern.

2. Following the inner outline, sew the additional rows, working from the inside toward the outside.

Embroider Neat Angles

To create neat right angles when working chain stitches, the trick is to sew a bit to the inside, as shown, when you turn the angle.

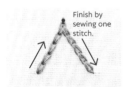

Finish by sewing one stitch.

Embroider Neat Circles

When creating a circle or an outline with chain stitches, make sure to connect the first and last stitches for a clean finish.

Bring the thread through the bottom of the first chain stitch.

Up

Down

Tips for Outline Stitches
Embroider Neat Curves

Bring the needle up and down, then back up halfway between the previous stitch, and repeat. To create an intricate curve, the trick is to make very fine stitches.

OK When working the needle back up halfway, bring it out above the previous stitch.

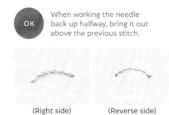

(Right side)   (Reverse side)

NO The curve will be imbalanced if the stitches are too big or don't come back up halfway.

(Right side)   (Reverse side)

Embroider Neat Angles

When creating right angles (or close-to-right angles) using outline stitches, pass the needle through a stitch on the reverse side to keep the thread from coming loose.

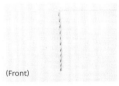

(Front)

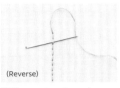

(Reverse)

(Reverse)

(Front)

1. Sew outline stitches to the corner.

2. When you turn the angle, pass the needle through a stitch on the reverse side.

3. Bring the needle up at the corner on the front side.

4. Continue sewing in the new direction.

Embroidering with Two Colors of Thread at a Time

By using strands in two different colors, the color looks variegated and creates a deeper effect.

1. Arrange the same lengths of the specified number of strands of each color of thread.

2. Pass the thread from step 1 through the needle. Tie a knot at one end of the thread. Embroider stitches as you normally would.

Neatening Your Fabric Edge

Neatening your fabric edge will prevent the edges from fraying while embroidering and will make your work go more smoothly.

High-count (fine) linen: Create a fringed edge on all four sides by gently unraveling the thread about a 1/4 inch on each side.

Low-count (coarse) linen: Sew a rough whipstitch on all sides, or use pinking shears to cut the fabric.

Transferring Patterns

First, locate the area where you will transfer the pattern to the fabric. Arrange the pattern along the warp and weft.

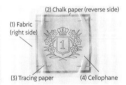

(2) Chalk paper (reverse side)

(1) Fabric (right side)

(3) Tracing paper   (4) Cellophane

1. Place the tracing paper over the pattern, and transfer.

2. Layer as shown in the photo, secure with pins, and trace the pattern using a tracer.

How to Handle Thread (1)

For No. 25 embroidery floss, pull the specified number of strands from the skein, one at a time, then arrange them together with the ends aligned neatly.

1. Pull a standard length of 24 inches from the skein and cut the thread.

2. One at a time, pull the number of strands you need, and arrange them together.

How to Handle Thread (2)

How you thread the desired number of strands through the needle differs depending on whether you're using an odd or even number of strands.

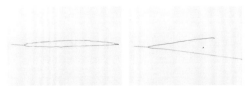

For even numbers of strands: for every 2 strands, thread 1 length through the needle, fold it in half, align the ends, then make a knot.

For odd numbers of strands: arrange the desired number of strands, thread the needle, and make a knot at one end.

Knots

Make a knot at the end of the thread when you start stitching embroidery for projects.

3. Pinch the wrapped thread between your fingertips, slide it down the needle, and pull the knot all the way to the end of the thread.

1. Thread the strands through the needle, place the end of the thread near the tip of the needle.

2. Wrap the thread twice around the tip of the needle.

Starting Your Embroidery (1)

Here's how to start embroidering when creating lines using chain or outline stitches.

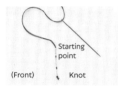 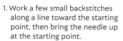 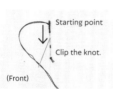

1. Work a few small backstitches along a line toward the starting point, then bring the needle up at the starting point.

2. Continue working, overlaying the stitches from step 1. When you reach the knot, clip it off.

Starting Your Embroidery (2)

Here's how to start embroidering when filling in areas using satin stitches.

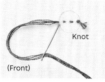 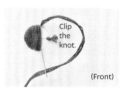

1. Work a few pick stitches (or short running stitches) along a line toward the starting point, then bring the needle up at the starting point.

2. Continue working, covering the stitches from step 1. When you reach the knot, clip it off.

Finishing Your Embroidery (1)

Here's how to finish embroidering once you've created lines using chain or outline stitches.

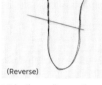 

1. Bring the needle up on the reverse side and anchor the thread by wrapping it through several times around a stitch on this side.

2. Cut the end of the thread.

Finishing Your Embroidery (2)

Here's how to finish embroidering once you've filled in areas using satin stitches.

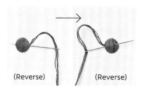 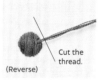

1. Bring the needle up on the reverse side, pass the thread under the stitches several times to anchor the thread.

2. Cut the end of the thread.

When Switching Thread

When you run out of thread or need to switch colors, start a new thread where stitches already exist.

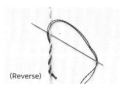

Weave a knotted length of thread around the stitches on the reverse side, and bring the needle up at the starting point. Cut off the knot later.

Completing Your Project

Once you've finished your project, be sure to treat and handle it carefully to help improve the appearance.

1. Erase any pattern traces. If the marks are water-soluble, mist water on the reverse side of the fabric, then erase any traces that stick out. Use a moistened cotton swab for tight areas.

2. Touch up with an iron. Use an iron on the reverse side to lightly touch up any wrinkles. Textural stitches are easily damaged, so spread a towel under the project first. Be careful—once ironed, any traces of the ink will become permanent!

60

Embroidery Pattern Book

This section will introduce you to the art of embroidery and the basic stitches and skills you need to create beautifully finished embroidery work. The 39 patterns and instructions on how to make the projects are included. I encourage you to pick and choose your favorite motifs from among them and use them as highlights in your embroidery projects.

*The number in parentheses is the number of strands, followed by the color code or name for the DMC No. 25 embroidery floss.

Monthly Emblems

Narcissus

page 6

- DMC No. 25 embroidery floss: 319, 522, 611, 613, 733, 3777, 3799, 3865
- Work chain stitch (2 strands), unless noted otherwise.
- Use 2 strands, unless noted otherwise.
- The number in parentheses is the number of strands, followed by the color code or name for the DMC No. 25 embroidery floss.

Plum Blossoms

page 10

- DMC No. 25 embroidery floss: 08, 611, 842, 844, 3371, 3831
- Work chain stitch (2 strands), unless noted otherwise.
- Use 2 strands, unless noted otherwise.
- The number in parentheses is the number of strands, followed by the color code or name for the DMC No. 25 embroidery floss.

Dandelions

page 14

- DMC No. 25 embroidery floss: 522, 611, 733, 986, 3866
- Work chain stitch (2 strands), unless noted otherwise.
- Use 2 strands, unless noted otherwise.
- The number in parentheses is the number of strands, followed by the color code or name for the DMC No. 25 embroidery floss.

French knot (6) 611

French knot 611

Outline 611

Outline 986

611

986

Straight (6) 733

3866

French knot (3) 733

522

986

Easter Bunny

page 18

- DMC No. 25 embroidery floss: 01, 08, 310, 733, 844, 895, 3033
- Work chain stitch (2 strands), unless noted otherwise.
- Use 2 strands, unless noted otherwise.
- The number in parentheses is the number of strands, followed by the color code or name for the DMC No. 25 embroidery floss.

Outline 733

French knot (6) 733

Work straight stitches 310 over chain stitches.

733

French knot 310

01

Leave a gap where the neck overlaps with the body.

3033

08

08

844

3033

Lazy daisy + straight (4) 895

Outline 08

Poppies

page 22

- DMC No. 25 embroidery floss: 501, 522, 611, 733, 920, 976, 3687, 3727, 3866
- Work chain stitch (2 strands), unless noted otherwise.
- Use 2 strands, unless noted otherwise.
- The number in parentheses is the number of strands, followed by the color code or name for the DMC No. 25 embroidery floss.

Lazy daisy + straight (4) 611

French knot (4) 611

Outline 611

611

920

3687

3727

976

3866

733

Long and short (6) *Use for all flower petals.

French knot (4) 3866 *Use for all flower centers.

733

920

3687

976

501

Outline 522

Rainy Season

page 26

- DMC No. 25 embroidery floss: 32, 169, 319, 611, 844, 3750, 3866
- Work chain stitch (2 strands), unless noted otherwise.
- Use 2 strands, unless noted otherwise.
- The number in parentheses is the number of strands, followed by the color code or name for the DMC No. 25 embroidery floss.

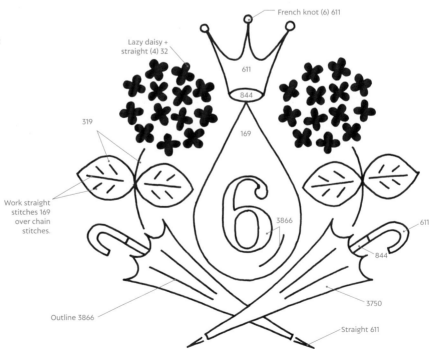

French knot (6) 611

Lazy daisy + straight (4) 32

611

844

319

169

Work straight stitches 169 over chain stitches.

3866

611

844

3750

Outline 3866

Straight 611

64

Coral and Shell

page 30

- DMC No. 25 embroidery floss:
  01, 03, 22, 543, 611, 844
- Work chain stitch (2 strands),
  unless noted otherwise.
- Use 2 strands, unless noted
  otherwise.
- The number in parentheses
  is the number of strands,
  followed by the color code
  or name for the DMC No. 25
  embroidery floss.

Lazy daisy + straight (4) 611

611

01   03

844

Outline 22

French knot 543

22

Work straight stitches 03
over chain stitches.

Pineapple

page 34

- DMC No. 25 embroidery floss:
  829, 833, 986, 3364, 3866
- Work chain stitch (2 strands),
  unless noted otherwise.
- Use 2 strands, unless noted
  otherwise.
- The number in parentheses is
  the number of strands, followed
  by the color code or name for
  the DMC No. 25 embroidery
  floss.

986

3364

833

Outline 986

3866

Work straight stitches (1)
829 over chain stitches.

Grapes

page 38

- DMC No. 25 embroidery floss: 29, 319, 611, 632, 733, 3371, 3866
- Work chain stitch (2 strands), unless noted otherwise.
- Use 2 strands, unless noted otherwise.
- The number in parentheses is the number of strands, followed by the color code or name for the DMC No. 25 embroidery floss.

French knot (6) 733

Outline 632

319

319

French knot (6) 29

3371

3866

611

Work straight stitches 3371 over chain stitches.

Pumpkin

page 42

- DMC No. 25 embroidery floss: 301, 611, 898, 935, 936, 3363, 3866
- Work chain stitch (2 strands), unless noted otherwise.
- Use 2 strands, unless noted otherwise.
- The number in parentheses is the number of strands, followed by the color code or name for the DMC No. 25 embroidery floss.

French knot (6) 611

Lazy daisy + straight (6) 3363

611

Outline 611

936

Work outline stitches 898 over chain stitches.

Outline 935

Outline 898

3866

935

301

936

3363

Work outline stitches 898 over chain stitches.

Teapot and Fallen Leaves

page 46

- DMC No. 25 embroidery floss: 300, 611, 632, 841, 3031, 3777, 3866
- Work chain stitch (2 strands), unless noted otherwise.
- Use 2 strands, unless noted otherwise.
- The number in parentheses is the number of strands, followed by the color code or name for the DMC No. 25 embroidery floss.

Lazy daisy + straight (4) 611

Outline 611

Work straight stitches 841 over chain stitches.

3777

611

632

3866

Work straight stitches 3031 over chain stitches.

841

3031

Outline (1) 3866

300

3777

Work straight stitches 841 over chain stitches.

Mistletoe

page 50

- DMC No. 25 embroidery floss: 501, 611, 733, 844, 3866
- Work chain stitch (2 strands), unless noted otherwise.
- Use 2 strands, unless noted otherwise.
- The number in parentheses is the number of strands, followed by the color code or name for the DMC No. 25 embroidery floss.

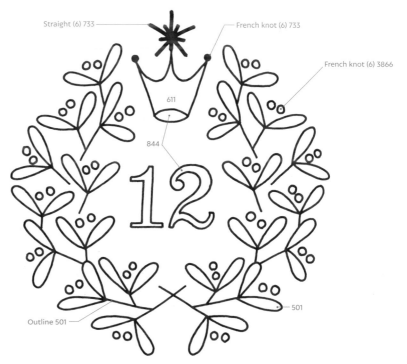

Straight (6) 733

French knot (6) 733

French knot (6) 3866

611

844

Outline 501

501

Spring Herbs

page 7

- DMC No. 25 embroidery floss: ecru, 367, 520, 611, 833, 3721
- Work chain stitch (2 strands), unless noted otherwise.
- Use 2 strands, unless noted otherwise.
- The number in parentheses is the number of strands, followed by the color code or name for the DMC No. 25 embroidery floss.

Enlarge by 110 percent

Work outline stitches (6) 611 over chain stitches.

367

Work outline stitches (6) ecru over chain stitches.

520

Straight (6) ecru

Work outline stitches (6) 611 over chain stitches.

367

Straight (6) 833

French knot (6) ecru

French knot (6) 833

Lazy daisy + straight (4) 520

Outline (6) 367

Ecru

Straight 611

Work outline stitches (6) 3721 over chain stitches.

520

3721

Lazy daisy + straight (4) 367

Straight (3) 520

French knot (6) ecru

Outline (3) 520

367

Lazy daisy + straight (6) 520

Ecru

Outline (3) 611

68

Happy New Year

page 8

- DMC No. 25 embroidery floss: 31, 407, 522, 561, 739, 834, 932, 976, 3350, 3750
- Work outline stitch for stems.
- Work chain stitch (2 strands), unless noted otherwise.
- Use 2 strands, unless noted otherwise.

- The number in parentheses is the number of strands, followed by the color code or name for the DMC No. 25 embroidery floss.

Enlarge by 110 percent

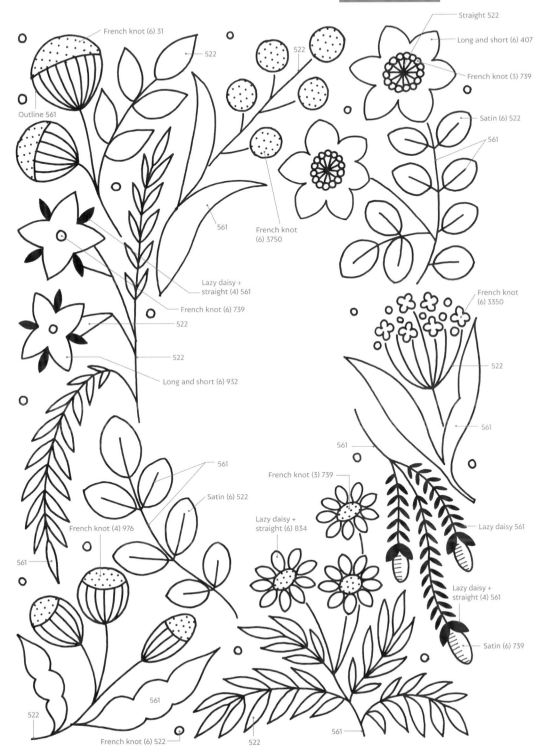

French knot (6) 31

522

522

Straight 522

Long and short (6) 407

French knot (3) 739

Outline 561

Satin (6) 522

561

561

French knot (6) 3750

French knot (6) 3350

Lazy daisy + straight (4) 561

French knot (6) 739

522

522

522

561

561

Long and short (6) 932

French knot (3) 739

Lazy daisy 561

561

561

561

Satin (6) 522

Lazy daisy + straight (6) 834

Lazy daisy + straight (4) 561

French knot (4) 976

Satin (6) 739

561

561

522

561

French knot (6) 522

522

Pansies

page 9

- DMC No. 25 embroidery floss: 168, 169, 733, 930, 3362, 3363
- Use 2 strands, unless noted otherwise.
- The number in parentheses is the number of strands, followed by the color code or name for the DMC No. 25 embroidery floss.

Satin (6) 930

French knot (4) 733

Work satin stitches 930 over long and short stitches.

Long and short (6) 168

Satin (6) 169

Satin 930

Chain 3363

Outline 3363

Outline (4) 3363

Satin (6) 3362

Spring Birds

page 11

- DMC No. 25 embroidery floss: ecru, 832, 840, 931, 3021, 3831
- Use 2 strands, unless noted otherwise.
- The number in parentheses is the number of strands, followed by the color code or name for the DMC No. 25 embroidery floss.

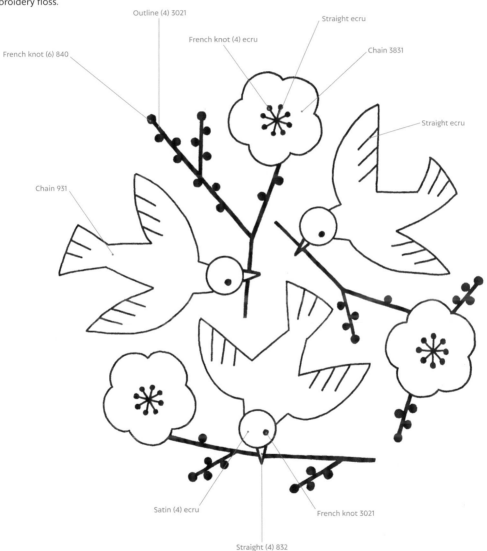

Outline (4) 3021

French knot (4) ecru

Straight ecru

Chain 3831

French knot (6) 840

Straight ecru

Chain 931

Satin (4) ecru

French knot 3021

Straight (4) 832

Bird and Plant Pattern

page 12

• DMC No. 25 embroidery floss: 168, 501, 502, 543, 647, 823, 3768, 3864

• Work chain stitch (2 strands), unless noted otherwise.

• Work outline stitch (4 strands) for stems, unless noted otherwise.

• The number in parentheses is the number of strands, followed by the color code or name for the DMC No. 25 embroidery floss.

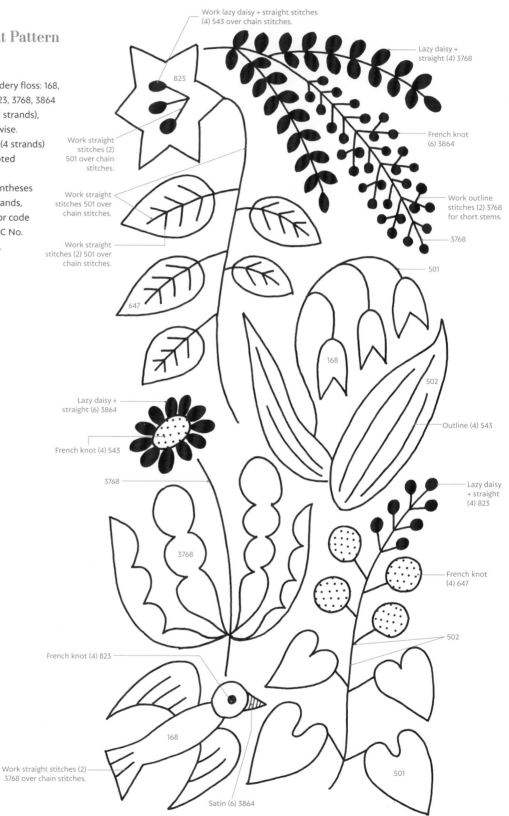

Work lazy daisy + straight stitches (4) 543 over chain stitches.

Lazy daisy + straight (4) 3768

French knot (6) 3864

Work outline stitches (2) 3768 for short stems.

3768

501

823

Work straight stitches (2) 501 over chain stitches.

Work straight stitches 501 over chain stitches.

Work straight stitches (2) 501 over chain stitches.

647

168

502

Outline (4) 543

Lazy daisy + straight (6) 3864

French knot (4) 543

3768

Lazy daisy + straight (4) 823

3768

French knot (4) 647

French knot (4) 823

502

168

501

Work straight stitches (2) 3768 over chain stitches.

Satin (6) 3864

Wine Bag

page 13

- DMC No. 25 embroidery floss: 3866
- Work chain stitch (2 strands) for thick lines and outline stitch (2 strands) for thin lines, unless noted otherwise.
- The number in parentheses is the number of strands.
- See page 93 for instructions for making the wine bag.

Enlarge by 200 percent

Lazy daisy + straight (4)

Lazy daisy + straight (4)

French knot (6)

Chain (2)

French knot (4)

Lazy daisy + straight (6)

Lazy daisy + straight (4)

Chain (2)

French knot (4)

French knot (4)

Chain (2)

French knot (4)

Tulips

page 15

- DMC No. 25 embroidery floss: ecru, 301, 610, 782, 832, 834, 986, 3052
- The number in parentheses is the number of strands, followed by the color code or name for the DMC No. 25 embroidery floss.

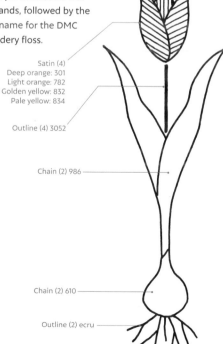

Satin (4)
Deep orange: 301
Light orange: 782
Golden yellow: 832
Pale yellow: 834

Outline (4) 3052

Chain (2) 986

Chain (2) 610

Outline (2) ecru

Mimosas

page 16, 17

- DMC No. 25 embroidery floss: 501, 502, 833
- The number in parentheses is the number of strands, followed by the color code or name for the DMC No. 25 embroidery floss.

French knot (6) 833

Straight (2) 502

Straight (6) 501

Outline (2) 502

Cherry-Blossom Viewing

page 19

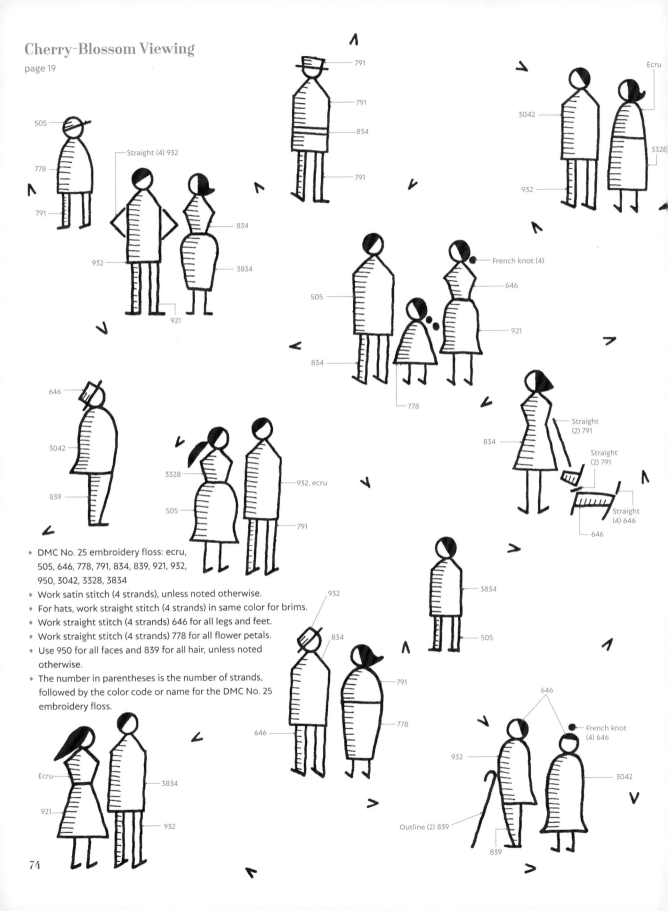

505

778

791

Straight (4) 932

932

921

834

3834

791

791

834

791

Ecru

3042

932

3328

505

834

778

French knot (4)

646

921

646

3042

839

3328

505

932, ecru

791

834

Straight
(2) 791

Straight
(2) 791

Straight
(4) 646

646

3834

505

• DMC No. 25 embroidery floss: ecru, 505, 646, 778, 791, 834, 839, 921, 932, 950, 3042, 3328, 3834

• Work satin stitch (4 strands), unless noted otherwise.

• For hats, work straight stitch (4 strands) in same color for brims.

• Work straight stitch (4 strands) 646 for all legs and feet.

• Work straight stitch (4 strands) 778 for all flower petals.

• Use 950 for all faces and 839 for all hair, unless noted otherwise.

• The number in parentheses is the number of strands, followed by the color code or name for the DMC No. 25 embroidery floss.

932

834

791

778

646

646

French knot
(4) 646

932

3042

Ecru

921

3834

932

Outline (2) 839

839

Spring Pressed Flowers

page 20

- DMC No. 25 embroidery floss: 08, 225, 319, 522, 561, 986, 3350, 3687, 3866
- Work chain stitch (2 strands), unless noted otherwise.
- Use 2 strands, unless noted otherwise.
- The number in parentheses is the number of strands, followed by the color code or name for the DMC No. 25 embroidery floss.

Wisteria Trellis Pattern

page 23

- DMC No. 25 embroidery floss: B5200, 520, 554, 718, 733, 791, 3607, 3862
- Work chain stitch (2 strands), unless noted otherwise.
- Use 2 strands, unless noted otherwise.
- The number in parentheses is the number of strands, followed by the color code or name for the DMC No. 25 embroidery floss.

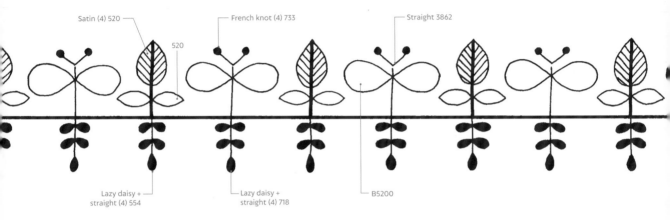

Satin (4) 520

520

French knot (4) 733

Straight 3862

Lazy daisy +
straight (4) 554

Lazy daisy +
straight (4) 718

B5200

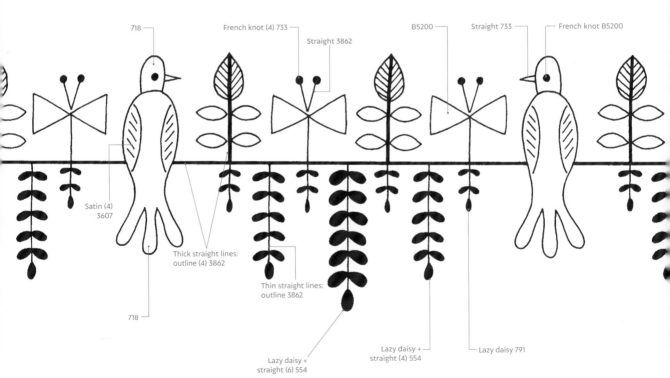

718

French knot (4) 733

Straight 3862

B5200

Straight 733

French knot B5200

Satin (4)
3607

Thick straight lines:
outline (4) 3862

718

Thin straight lines:
outline 3862

Lazy daisy +
straight (6) 554

Lazy daisy +
straight (4) 554

Lazy daisy 791

Fresh Green Wreath

page 25

- DMC No. 25 embroidery floss: 319, 520, 3022, 3024, 3363
- Work outline stitch (2) for stems and straight stitch (2) for short stems.
- Work chain stitch (2 strands), unless noted otherwise.
- The number in parentheses is the number of strands, followed by the color code or name for the DMC No. 25 embroidery floss.

3363

319

French knot (6) 3022

Satin (4) 520

3022

Lazy daisy + straight (2) 3022

319

Lazy daisy + straight (4) 3024

520   520

French knot (6) 3363

3363

French knot (4) 520

3363

3022

Spring Flower Pattern

page 24

- DMC No. 25 embroidery floss: 22, 29, 336, 733, 739, 895, 3042, 3363, 3865
- Work outline stitch (2 strands) for stems.
- Work chain stitch (2 strands), unless noted otherwise.
- The number in parentheses is the number of strands, followed by the color code or name for the DMC No. 25 embroidery floss.

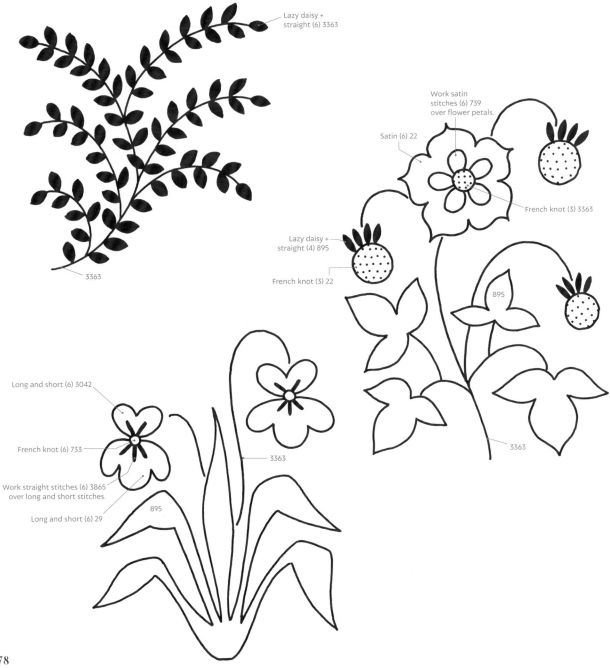

Lazy daisy + straight (6) 3363

Work satin stitches (6) 739 over flower petals.

Satin (6) 22

French knot (3) 3363

Lazy daisy + straight (4) 895

French knot (3) 22

3363

895

3363

Long and short (6) 3042

French knot (6) 733

Work straight stitches (6) 3865 over long and short stitches.

Long and short (6) 29

895

3363

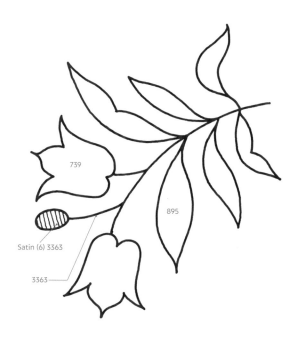

739

895

Satin (6) 3363

3363

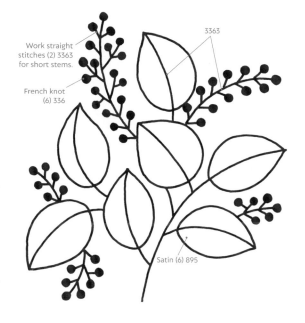

Work straight
stitches (2) 3363
for short stems.

French knot
(6) 336

3363

Satin (6) 895

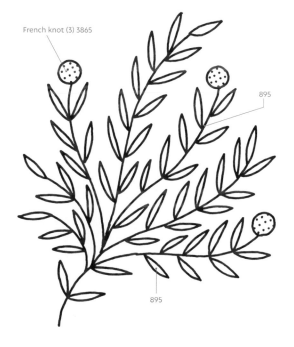

French knot (3) 3865

895

895

Long and short (6) 3865

French knot
(3) 733

895

3363

Hydrangea

page 27

+ DMC No. 25 embroidery floss: 336, 543, 733
+ The number in parentheses is the number of strands, followed by the color code or name for the DMC No. 25 embroidery floss.

Lazy daisy + straight (6) 543

Outline (2) 336

Straight (1) 733

French knot (2) 733

School of Fish

page 31

+ DMC No. 25 embroidery floss: 3866
+ Work outline stitch (2), unless noted otherwise.
+ The number in parentheses is the number of strands.

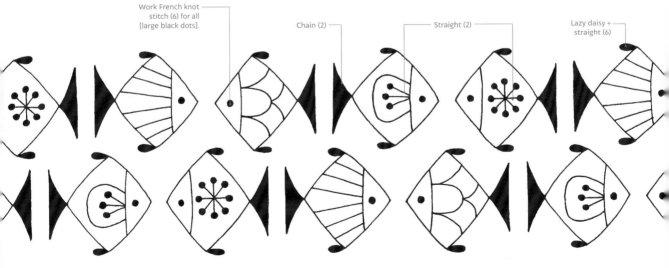

Work French knot stitch (6) for all [large black dots].

Chain (2)

Straight (2)

Lazy daisy + straight (6)

Lavender

page 28

Eye Mask

page 29

- DMC No. 25 embroidery floss: 29, 501, 502
- The number in parentheses is the number of strands, followed by the color code or name for the DMC No. 25 embroidery floss.
- See page 94 for instructions for making the eye mask.

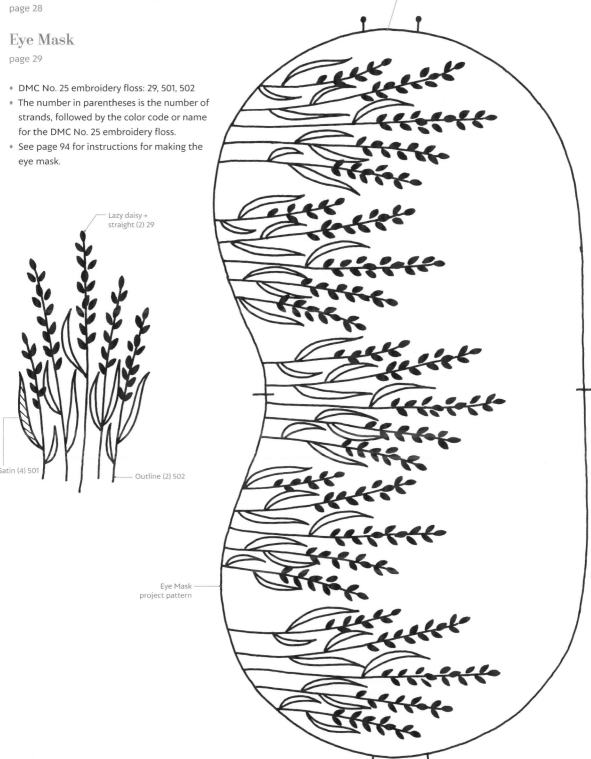

Attach band here.

Lazy daisy + straight (2) 29

Satin (4) 501

Outline (2) 502

Eye Mask project pattern

Surfers
page 32, 33

3790

833

3790

794

Work straight stitches (2)
3866 over chain stitches.

Outline (2) 3866

22

841

839

841

991

Work straight stitches (2)
833 over chain stitches.

3750

833

543

991

543

Satin (4) 22

839

543

Work straight stitches (2)
794 over chain stitches.

833

543

3750

Outline (2) 3866

839

841

841

Work straight stitches (2)
3866 over chain stitches.

22

794

3790

833

Satin (4) 794

3790

Outline (2) 3750

3866

991

- ◆ DMC No. 25 embroidery floss:
  22, 543, 794, 833, 839, 841, 991,
  3750, 3790, 3866
- ◆ Work satin stitch (4 strands)
  for faces and hair.
- ◆ Work chain stitch (2 strands),
  unless noted otherwise.
- ◆ The number in parentheses
  is the number of strands,
  followed by the color
  code or name for the DMC
  No. 25 embroidery floss.

Work straight stitches (2)
839 over chain stitches.

3790

Tropical Leaves

page 35

French knot (4) 3012

Outline (2) 561

Work lazy daisy + straight stitches (4) 644 over chain stitches.

Outline (2) 500

502

644

647

632

Outline (2) 500

500

502

561

611

Work 611 over chain stitches.

561

502

Work straight stitches (4) 644 over chain stitches.

Work 644 over chain stitches.

500

839

- DMC No. 25 embroidery floss: 500, 502, 561, 611, 632, 644, 647, 839, 3012
- Work outline stitch (4 strands) for thick lines; for all other stitches, work chain stitch (2 strands), unless noted otherwise.
- The number in parentheses is the number of strands, followed by the color code or name for the DMC No. 25 embroidery floss.

Work straight stitches (4) 644 over chain stitches.

644

611

Summer Fruits

page 36, 37

- DMC No. 25 embroidery floss: 22, 29, 301, 522, 561, 733, 739, 3021, 3687, 3865
- Work outline stitch (4 strands) 3021 for all fruit stems.

- Work chain stitch (2 strands), unless noted otherwise.
- The number in parentheses is the number of strands, followed by the color code or name for the DMC No. 25 embroidery floss.

Work straight stitches (4) 3865 over chain stitches.

Outline (2) 3865

739

561

733

561

522

561

3687

Work straight stitches (2) 3021 over chain stitches.

733

Work lazy daisy + straight stitches (4) 3021 over chain stitches.

739

3865

French knot (2) 22

Work straight stitches (4) 3021 over chain stitches.

3865

561

Work straight stitches (4) 739 over chain stitches.

Satin (6) 522

733

522

3021

301

Satin (6) 29

733

Straight (6) 561

Straight (4) 3021

3687

Satin (6) 29

Satin (6) 733

22

739

301

3865

733

Work French knot stitches (4) 3021 over chain stitches.

Satin (6) 522

Work straight stitches (4) 739 over chain stitches.

3865

561

Satin (6) 522

Satin (6) 561

522

522

561

561

522

Work straight stitches (4) 739 over chain stitches.

561

733

3865

561

Work straight stitches (4) 3021 over chain stitches.

522

Satin (6) 3687

Work straight stitches (4) 3865 over chain stitches.

Satin (6) 3687

84

Purple Flowers

page 39

- ◆ DMC No. 25 embroidery floss: 29, 936, 937, 3041, 3740, 3865
- ◆ For stems, work outline stitch (6 strands) for thick lines and outline stitch (2 strands) for thin lines.
- ◆ For all other stitches, work chain stitch (2 strands), unless noted otherwise.
- ◆ The number in parentheses is the number of strands, followed by the color code or name for the DMC No. 25 embroidery floss.

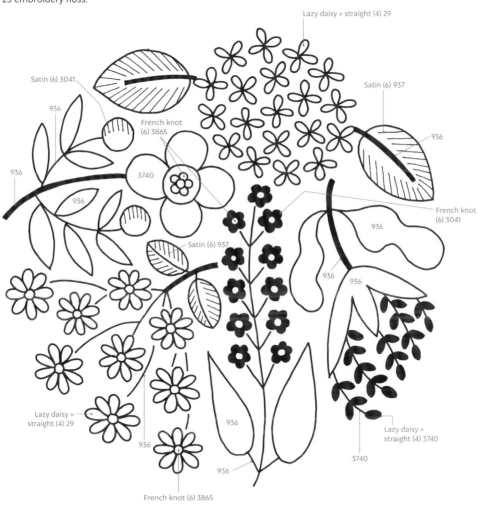

Autumn Fruits

page 40, 41

- DMC No. 25 embroidery floss: 150, 154, 522, 648, 902, 3021, 3042, 3362, 3866
- Work chain stitch (2 strands), unless noted otherwise.
- Use 2 strands, unless noted otherwise.
- The number in parentheses is the number of strands, followed by the color code or name for the DMC No. 25 embroidery floss.

Outline (4) 3021

Outline 3021

Satin (4) 3362

French knot 648

Outline 522

French knot (6) 154

522

Work outline stitches 3021 over chain stitches.

Work outline stitches (4) 3021 over chain stitches.

3362

Work outline stitches 154 over chain stitches.

902

902

Outline 3021

French knot (4) 150

3866

Lazy daisy + straight 3362

Outline 3362

Outline (4) 3021

Satin (4) 3362

French knot (4) 648

150

Outline (4) 3866

3042

Lazy daisy + straight (6) 522

Outline (4) 3021

Outline 3362
* Work straight stitches for short lines.

Lazy daisy + straight (6) 3362

Mushroom Wreath

page 43

- DMC No. 25 embroidery floss: ecru, 300, 422, 646, 832, 839, 869, 890, 920, 3041, 3371, 3777
- Work chain stitch (2 strands), unless noted otherwise.
- Use 2 strands, unless noted otherwise.
- For mushroom caps, work patterns over chain stitches.
- The number in parentheses is the number of strands, followed by the color code or name for the DMC No. 25 embroidery floss.

French knot ecru

869

Straight 3371

Satin (4) 832

Straight 646

832

Ecru

3041

Outline 890

Ecru

Outline 646

Lazy daisy +
straight 890

Outline (4) 890
*Work same for all grasses.

422

French knot (4) 839

3371

Ecru

646

Satin (4) 839

French knot (4) ecru

3777

Straight 3371

Outline (4) 890
*Work same for all mushroom gills.

Ecru

300

300

Ecru

French knot ecru

Outline ecru

422

3371

920

422

Straight 646

869

Ecru

French knot 422

839

422

890

Straight (4) 646
* Work same for all mushroom fibers.

Camping Gear

page 44

* DMC No. 25 embroidery floss: 310, 355, 612, 646, 780, 801, 833, 890, 926, 3031, 3865
* Work chain stitch (2 strands), unless noted otherwise.
* The number in parentheses is the number of strands, followed by the color code or name for the DMC No. 25 embroidery floss.

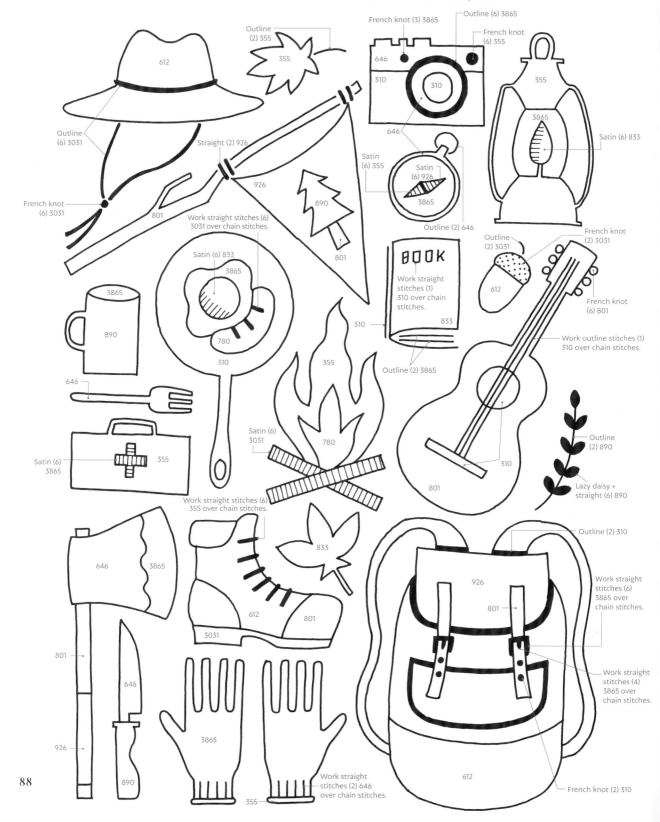

Pear and Flower Pattern

page 45

- DMC No. 25 embroidery floss: 610, 832, 936, 3012, 3021, 3033
- Work outline stitch (2 strands), unless noted otherwise.
- The number in parentheses is the number of strands, followed by the color code or name for the DMC No. 25 embroidery floss.

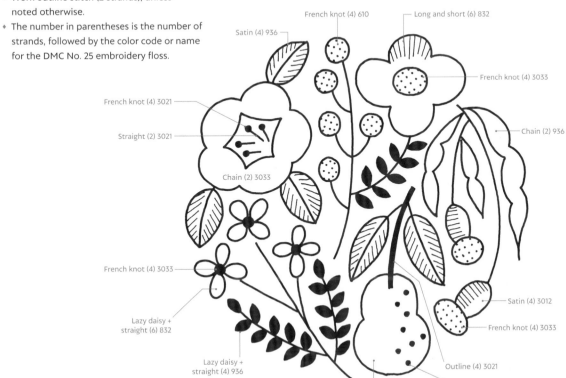

Satin (4) 936
French knot (4) 610
Long and short (6) 832
French knot (4) 3033
French knot (4) 3021
Straight (2) 3021
Chain (2) 936
Chain (2) 3033
French knot (4) 3033
Satin (4) 3012
French knot (4) 3033
Lazy daisy + straight (6) 832
Outline (4) 3021
Lazy daisy + straight (4) 936
Chain (2) 832
French knot (4) 3033

Migratory Birds

page 47

- DMC No. 25 embroidery floss: ecru
- Work outline stitch (2 strands), unless noted otherwise.
- The number in parentheses is the number of strands.

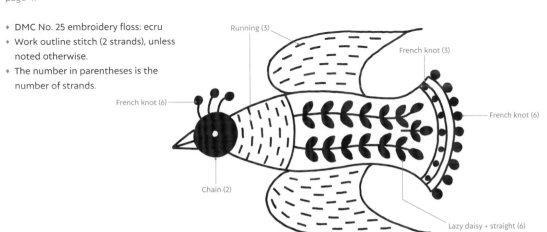

Running (3)
French knot (3)
French knot (6)
French knot (6)
Chain (2)
Lazy daisy + straight (6)

Sewing Tools

page 48, 49

• DMC No. 25 embroidery floss: 310, 561, 611, 648, 739, 833, 930, 932, 3031, 3777, 3799, 3834, 3866
• Work outline stitch (6 strands) for thick lines; however, work straight stitch for thin lines.
• Work French knot stitch for all [large black dots].

• For all other stitches, work chain stitch (2 strands), unless noted otherwise.
• The number in parentheses is the number of strands, followed by the color code or name for the DMC No. 25 embroidery floss.

Enlarge by 110 percent

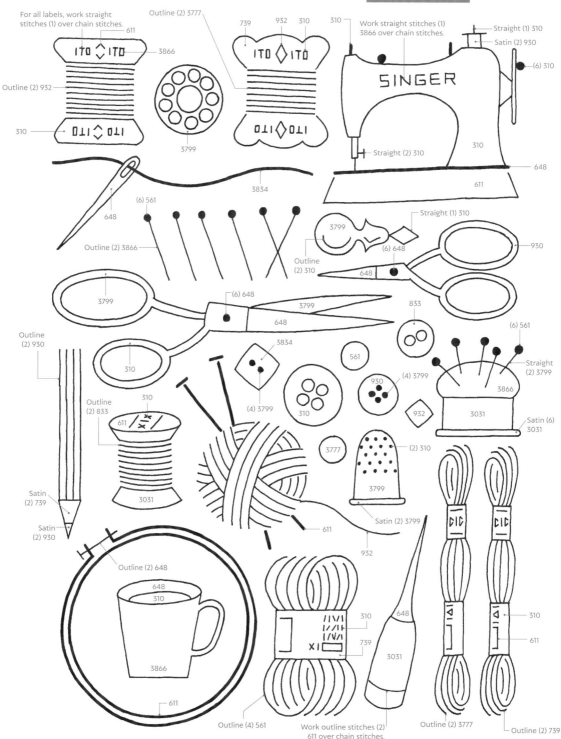

For all labels, work straight stitches (1) over chain stitches.

Outline (2) 3777

Outline (2) 932

611

3866

310

739 932 310

Work straight stitches (1) 3866 over chain stitches.

Straight (1) 310
Satin (2) 930
(6) 310

SINGER

310

Straight (2) 310

648

611

3799

3834

648

Outline (2) 3866

(6) 561

3799

3799

Outline (2) 310

3799

(6) 648

648

Straight (1) 310

930

648

833

(6) 561

Straight (2) 3799

Outline (2) 930

310

Outline (2) 833

310

611

3834

(4) 3799

561

930

(4) 3799

932

3866

3031

Satin (6) 3031

Satin (2) 739

3031

310

3777

(2) 310

3799

Satin (2) 3799

Satin (2) 930

Outline (2) 648

648
310

3866

611

932

611

Outline (4) 561

310

739

648

3031

Work outline stitches (2) 611 over chain stitches.

Outline (2) 3777

310

611

Outline (2) 739

Snow Flower Pattern

page 51

- DMC No. 25 embroidery floss: 640, 815, 890, 3021, 3046, 3047, 3345, 3768, 3787
- Use 6 strands, unless noted otherwise.
- The number in parentheses is the number of strands, followed by the color code or name for the DMC No. 25 embroidery floss.

Enlarge by 110 percent

French knot 3768

French knot 640

Satin (4) 3046

Satin 3047

Satin 3345

Satin 890

Satin 3787

Outline (3) 3021

Chain (2) 3345

Lazy daisy (2) 890

French knot 815

French knot 815

Lazy daisy + straight 3047

French knot (4) 3768

Straight (2) 3768

Christmas Rose

page 52

Christmas Stocking

page 53

- DMC No. 25 embroidery floss: 319, 733, 3866
- Work outline stitch (2 strands) 319, unless noted otherwise.
- The number in parentheses is the number of strands, followed by the color code or name for the DMC No. 25 embroidery floss.

Enlarge by 110 percent

Satin (6) 3866

French knot (6) 733

Lazy daisy + straight (4) 319

Christmas Stocking project pattern
*See page 95 for instructions for making the Christmas stocking.

Straight (2) 319
*Use for all short lines.

French knot (3) 3866

Lazy daisy + straight (6) 3866

Wine Bag

page 13

FINISHED SIZE
3¼" x 3¼" x 14" (main part of bag)

NO. 25 EMBROIDERY FLOSS
DMC 3866, 3 skeins

MATERIALS
Exterior fabric: linen, light gray, 33½" x 8"
Lining fabric: linen, white, 33½" x 8"
Handle fabric: linen, light gray, 11¾" x 4"
⅛"-wide faux leather cord, brown, 19¾",
  2 pieces
Machine-sewing thread, light gray, as needed

HOW TO MAKE

1

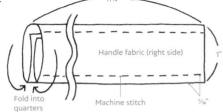

1. Using an iron, press folds into the fabric for the
   handle, as shown, and machine stitch both edges.

2

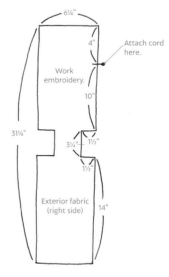

2. Transfer the embroidery pattern (p. 73), evenly spaced,
   onto the right side of the front exterior of the bag.
   Embroider the pattern, and iron your work lightly. Trace
   the finished dimensions onto the reverse side, as shown,
   and cut the fabric, adding a ½-inch seam allowance on all
   four sides. Cut the lining fabric to the same dimensions.

3

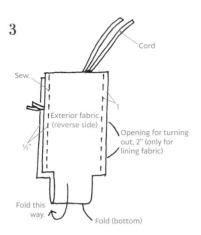

3. Fold the exterior fabric from step 2 in
   half with right sides together. Insert the
   two lengths of cord between the pieces
   of fabric at the attachment mark, and
   sew sides together. Sew the lining fabric
   in the same way, leaving an opening for
   turning out.

4

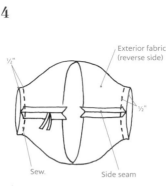

4. Press open the seam allowances on both
   sides of the exterior bag, then flatten the
   side seams in order to sew the edges of
   the bottom together. Repeat with the
   interior bag.

5

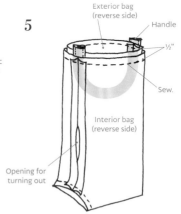

5. Assemble the exterior bag and interior
   bag from step 4 with right sides together.
   Insert the fabric for the handle from step 1
   on each side, in between the exterior and
   interior bags, and sew all the way around
   the mouth of the bag. Sew around once more to
   reinforce the handle.

6. Turn right side out, and lightly iron to
   reshape. With a U-shaped ladder stitch, sew
   the opening closed.

Eye Mask

page 29

FINISHED SIZE

7½" x 4"

NO. 25 EMBROIDERY FLOSS

DMC 29, 501, 502, about 1 skein each

MATERIALS

Exterior fabric: linen, beige, 10" x 6", 2 pieces
Quilt batting, 10" x 6"
Band fabric: linen, beige, 1½" x 18½"
¼"-mm-wide elastic, brown, 13¾"
Machine-sewing thread, beige, as needed

TOOLS

Bodkin

HOW TO MAKE

1. Fold the fabric for the band with right sides together, as shown, and sew edge. Turn right side out, and use the bodkin to thread the elastic through, then sew edges closed.

2. Transfer the embroidery pattern, evenly spaced, onto the right side of one piece of exterior fabric. Embroider the pattern, and iron your work lightly. Trace the finished dimensions of the project pattern (p. 81) onto the reverse side and cut the fabric, adding a ½-inch seam allowance all around.

3. Cut the second piece of exterior fabric and the quilt batting to the same dimensions as the piece from step 2. Assemble both pieces of the exterior fabric with right sides together, with the band from step 1 inserted in between, then place over the quilt batting, as shown, and sew together all around, leaving an opening for turning out.

4. Trim the excess fabric from the seam allowance, leaving a ¼-inch seam allowance, and make cuts along the curves.

5. Turn right side out, and lightly iron to reshape. With a U-shaped ladder stitch, sew the opening closed.

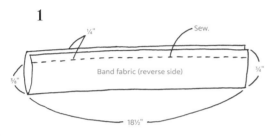

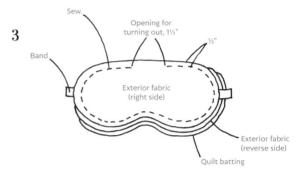

Cushion

page 33

FINISHED SIZE

17¾" x 17¾"

DMC NO. 25 EMBROIDERY FLOSS

Refer to pattern on page 82.

MATERIALS

Exterior fabric: linen, navy blue, 41¼" x 19¾"
Pillow insert, 17¾" x 17¾", 1 piece
Machine-sewing thread, navy blue, as needed

HOW TO MAKE

1. Cut exterior fabric to a size of 41¼" x 19¾". Transfer the embroidery patterns (p. 82) onto the right side of exterior fabric. Embroider the pattern, and iron your work lightly.

2. Using an iron, press ⅝" folds along the shorter edges of the fabric, as shown, and sew along edges.

3. With right side facing down, fold into thirds at marks shown in step 1, and sew the top and bottom edges together.

4. Turn inside out and reshape, then sew the top and bottom edges together again. Turn right side out, and lightly iron to reshape. Insert pillow insert.

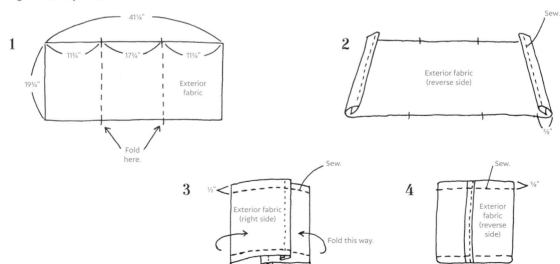

Cover

page 37

FINISHED SIZE
5½" diameter

DMC NO. 25 EMBROIDERY FLOSS
Refer to pattern on page 84.

MATERIALS
Fabric: linen, beige, 6" x 6"
Your choice of string, 19¾"
*To fit a 3"-diameter lid

HOW TO MAKE

1. Draw a 5½"-diameter circle and transfer the
   embroidery pattern (p. 84), centered, onto the
   right side of the fabric. Embroider the pattern, and
   iron your work lightly.

2. Cut out the circle from step 1, place over the lid
   of the glass jar, and fasten by tying the string
   around it.

Christmas Stocking

page 53

FINISHED SIZE
Approximately 6½" x 9¼"

DMC NO. 25 EMBROIDERY FLOSS
Refer to pattern on page 92.

MATERIALS
Exterior fabric: linen, light blue, 8" x 11¾",
    2 pieces
Lining fabric: linen, white, 8" x 11¾", 2 pieces
Machine-sewing thread, light blue, as needed
Your choice of ribbon or string, 19¾"

HOW TO MAKE

1. Transfer the embroidery pattern (p. 92), evenly
   spaced, onto the right side of one piece of exterior
   fabric. Embroider the pattern, and iron your work
   lightly. Trace the finished dimensions of the project
   pattern (p. 92) onto the reverse side and cut the
   fabric, adding a ½" seam allowance all around. Cut
   the second piece of exterior fabric and the lining
   fabric to the same dimensions.

2. Assemble both pieces of the exterior fabric with
   right sides together, and sew around the edge,
   leaving the mouth open. Repeat with the lining
   fabric, leaving an opening for turning out on one
   side. Make cuts along the curves of the seam
   allowances for both.

3. Assemble the exterior bag and interior bag from
   step 2 with right sides together, and sew all the
   way around the mouth of the bag.

4. Turn right side out, and lightly iron to reshape.
   With a U-shaped ladder stitch, sew the opening
   closed. To hang stocking, fold ribbon or string in
   half and sew onto mouth of bag.

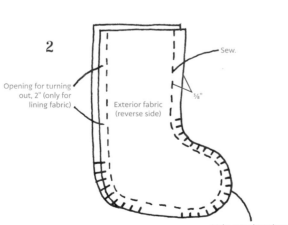

2

Opening for turning
out, 2" (only for
lining fabric)

Exterior fabric
(reverse side)

Sew.

⅜"

Make cuts along the curve.
*Do the same for lining fabric.

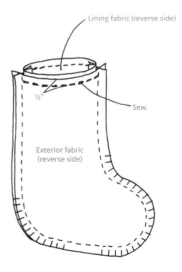

3

Lining fabric (reverse side)

½"

Exterior fabric
(reverse side)

Sew.

Yumiko Higuchi

After graduating from Tama Art University, Yumiko Higuchi worked as a handbag designer. Her pieces were shown and sold in boutiques. She began creating embroidery designs in 2008. She produces original embroidery patterns that feature botanical motifs and all manner of insects and living creatures.

ROOST BOOKS
An imprint of Shambhala Publications, Inc.
2129 13th Street
Boulder, Colorado 80302
www.shambhala.com

Translation © 2023 by Shambhala Publications, Inc.
Translation by Allison Markin Powell
Originally published as *Kisetsu no sutecchi*
© 2020 by Yumiko Higuchi
Educational Foundation Bunka Gakuen Bunka Publishing Bureau
English translation rights arranged with Educational Foundation Bunka Gakuen, Bunka Publishing Bureau through Japan UNI Agency, Inc., Tokyo

BUNKA PUBLISHING BUREAU STAFF CREDITS
Book Design: Hideyuki Saito
Photography: Shinsaku Kato
Styling: Kaori Maeda
Hair and Makeup: KOMAKI (nomadica)
Model: Catherine L. (AVOCADO)
Proofreader: Masako Mukai
Editors: Mariko Tsuchiya (Three Season); Kaori Tanaka (Bunka Publishing Bureau)
Publisher: Katsuhiro Hamada

Parts of this book appeared in a series featured in *Misesu* magazine, from January to December 2017, forming the basis for these contents, which have been updated and expanded.

9 8 7 6 5 4 3 2

Printed in China

Shambhala Publications makes every effort to print on acid-free, recycled paper.
Roost Books is distributed worldwide by Penguin Random House, Inc., and its subsidiaries.

LIBRARY OF CONGRESS CATALOGING-IN-PUBLICATION DATA
Names: Higuchi, Yumiko, 1975– author. | Powell, Allison Markin, translator.
Title: Stitching through the seasons: evocative patterns and projects to capture the magic of each month / Yumiko Higuchi; translation by Allison Markin Powell.
Other titles: Kisetsu no sutecchi. English
Description: Boulder: Shambhala, 2023. | Translation of: Kisetsu no sutecchi.
Identifiers: LCCN 2023001777 | ISBN 9781645471837 (trade paperback)
Subjects: LCSH: Embroidery—Patterns. | Seasons—Miscellanea.
Classification: LCC TT773.H54313 2023 | DDC 746.44041—dc23/eng/20230217
LC record available at https://lccn.loc.gov/2023001777